GEORGE ORWELL

George Orwell, whose real name was Eric Blair, was born in 1903. He won a scholarship to Eton then served in the Imperial Police in Burma from 1922-27, where his experiences of colonialism stayed with him for life.

His first book, *Down and Out in Paris and London* (1933), described his experiences in both cities of living on the poverty line. In *The Road to Wigan Pier* (1937) he wrote about the unemployed in the North of England, but before it was published he left for Spain and fought for the Republicans in the Civil War, as described in his *Homage to Catalonia* (1938).

He had by then also written three realistic novels, but it was the allegorical *Animal Farm* in 1945 that won him widespread acclaim, which was redoubled with the publication in 1949, just before his death the following year, of his most famous novel, *1984*.

IAN WOOLDRIDGE

Ian Wooldridge is a freelance director and acting teacher.

He was Artistic Director of the Royal Lyceum Theatre Company, Edinburgh, and TAG Theatre Company, based at the Citizens' Theatre in Glasgow. Read more at www.ian-wooldridge.com

Other Titles in this Series

George Orwell's

ANIMAL FARM

adapted by
IAN WOOLDRIDGE

NICK HERN BOOKS
London

www.nickhernbooks.co.uk

A Nick Hern Book

This stage adaptation of *Animal Farm* was first published in Great
Britain as a paperback original in 2004 by Nick Hern Books Limited,
14 Larden Road, London W3 7ST

© Ian Wooldridge and The Estate of Sonia Brownell Orwell 2004
Based on *Animal Farm* © The Estate of Sonia Brownell Orwell 1946

Cover image © Digital Vision

Typeset by Country Setting, Kingsdown, Kent, CT14 8ES
Printed and bound in Great Britain by Athenaeum Press Ltd,
Gateshead, Tyne and Wear

A CIP catalogue record for this book is available from
the British Library

ISBN 1 85459 789 2

For the invisible cat,
wherever she is!

PRODUCTION NOTES

When I adapted *Animal Farm* for the stage, I was working as
Artistic Director of a small-scale touring company, based in
Glasgow. In the first production, the Commandments were
written on a blackboard, and the animals existed in a world
that was part playground, part circus, but most of all, a
farmyard of the imagination. Audiences were made up mainly
of young people, many of whom knew little or nothing about
Soviet history, yet they immediately identified with the story,
characters, their relationships and situation. In discussions after
the show, the leading pigs were readily identified with
politicians of the day, and subsequent productions in the UK
and abroad have provoked audiences to similar reactions of
amusement and shock. Nothing stays the same, but, as *Animal
Farm* reminds us, one thing remains constant – the pigs will
always be there, snouts in the trough, looking up every now
and then, and eyeing the farmhouse greedily.

Staging

This adaptation was written for a company with limited
resources and a commitment to touring in theatres and schools.
This meant that the challenge of presenting the 'set-piece'
events of the story – in particular the Revolution, the Battle of
the Cowshed, Snowball's expulsion, the building of the windmill
and Boxer's departure – had to be met with solutions that
were imaginative, simple, yet theatrically effective. Subsequent
productions have involved a rich variety of presentation. For
the Revolution, a puppet was used for Mr Jones, wrapped in
red silk and tossed into oblivion, or savagely beaten and almost
drowned in a bath of water. The windmill has been a towering
edifice of suitcases, umbrellas and wooden pallets, a shining
silver construction of air-conditioning ducts, and large

children's building blocks piled high by the actors using only their fists and feet. Generally the set-pieces have been underscored with music, both live and recorded.

Ultimately it is for each company to decide how they will stage these spectacles. Directors, designers, actors, musicians, technicians, composers and choreographers will all have input to determine what works best in a given set of circumstances. Simplicity is the key, and people plus imagination, rather than elaborate resources, will always produce the best results. When the going gets tough, as it inevitably will, when the trial and error process of rehearsal doesn't seem to be getting anywhere, that is the time to go back to the original story for ideas and inspiration.

Costume and Movement

Depending on the style of the production, costumes should be minimal, in order to allow maximum movement, freedom and physical expression. What the actors wear does not have to represent the animals in any way. Masks and 'tails' are not necessary. Each actor has to create and express the essence of their animal in movement and sound. So, for example, the pigs might move on their toes whilst the horses are more flat-footed. Arms and hands become wings and tails. Animal sounds, which can have much in common with those of humans, are expressed freely throughout – the horses snort and whinny, the raven squawks, the donkey brays and the pigs grunt. When Napoleon and Squealer walk on 'two legs' and the Pigs/Men emerge for the final encounter with Pilkington, costume may be used to create the right image – they can walk on stilts, or in high platform boots, and wear elaborate or ridiculous 'human' clothes, unseen before. The moment should be truly shocking and it is for the actors, using their physical skills, to find its comical menace.

Ultimately, observation and practice are the best methods for realizing the animals. Plus, of course, constantly returning to the original fairy story in search of clues.

Casting

This version of *Animal Farm* was originally written for a company of six actors, but it can accommodate many more according to the needs of each production.

For a company of six, the division of parts could be as follows:

Actor 1	Major / Boxer / Young Animal
Actor 2	Squealer
Actor 3	Napoleon
Actor 4	Snowball / Benjamin
Actor 5	Clover
Actor 6	Moses / Mollie / Minimus / Pilkington

All other parts – sheep, dogs, pigeons, geese and hens – can be played by members of the company or, with larger numbers, by individual actors. The types of animal spreading rumours about Snowball (page 21) are entirely the decision of the company. The Young Animal has frequently been played as a puppy but other choices will work just as well.

The Storyteller can be divided amongst all the actors. Mr Jones does not speak, and in the original production was represented by a life-sized puppet. However, he can be performed by an actor, who might then play Pilkington at the end.

Whilst it is probably a good idea to have Boxer played by a man, and Clover and Mollie by women, all the other parts can be played by actors of either sex.

Thanks to Alan Lyddiard of Northern Stage, Newcastle, and Ivan Heng of Wild Rice Theatre Company, Singapore, for believing in it and making it happen; to the schools and youth theatres who staged it with imagination and flair; and to Nick Hern and Nicki Stoddart for getting it on the page.

I.W.

This adaptation of *Animal Farm* was first performed by
TAG Theatre Company at the Citizens' Theatre, Glasgow,
in March 1982.

The cast was Tam Dean Burn, Steve Owen, Patricia Ross,
Robin Sneller, Vari Sylvester and Laurie Ventry.

Directed by Ian Wooldridge

Animal Farm was revived by Northern Stage at the Gulbenkian
Studio Theatre, Newcastle-upon-Tyne, in February 1993,
and subsequently toured throughout the UK and Europe.

The cast was Janine Birkett, Maria Carrigan, Alan Lyddiard,
Tony Neilson, Derek Walmsley, David Whitaker and Tracey
Wilkinson.

Directed by Alan Lyddiard
Designed by Cath Hieatt
Lighting by Peter Barlow
Music by Test Department, Billy Bragg, David Whitaker
Choreography by Frank McConnell

Animal Farm was also performed by Wild Rice Theatre
Company in Singapore in April 2002, directed by Ivan Heng.

ANIMAL FARM

A Fairy Story

Characters

STORYTELLER

The Pigs

MAJOR
NAPOLEON
SQUEALER
SNOWBALL
MINIMUS

The Horses

BOXER
CLOVER
MOLLIE

BENJAMIN, *a donkey*

MOSES, *a raven*

YOUNG ANIMAL

The Farmers

MR JONES (*non-speaking*)
PILKINGTON

Assorted PIGS, PIGEONS, DOGS, GEESE, SHEEP, HENS

STORYTELLER. Mr Jones of the Manor Farm locked the
   hen-houses for the night, but was too drunk to remember
   to shut the pop-holes. With the ring of light from his lantern
   dancing from side to side, he lurched across the yard, drew
   himself a last glass of beer from the barrel in the scullery,
   and fell asleep in his armchair, alongside Mrs Jones.

   As soon as the light went out there was a stirring and a
   fluttering all through the farm. Word had gone round during
   the day that old Major the prize Middle White boar had
   had a strange dream on the previous night and wished to
   communicate it to the other animals.

MAJOR. Comrades, you have heard already about the
   strange dream that I had last night. But I will come to
   the dream later. I have something else to say first. I do
   not think, comrades, that I shall be with you for many
   months longer, and before I die, I feel it my duty to pass
   on to you such wisdom as I have acquired. I have had a
   long life, I have had much time for thought and I think
   I may say that I understand the nature of life on this earth
   as well as any animal now living. It is about this that
   I wish to speak to you.

   Now, comrades, what is the nature of this life of ours? Let
   us face it: our lives are miserable, laborious and short.
   We are born, we are given just so much food as will keep
   the breath in our bodies. Those of us who are capable of it
   are forced to work to the last atom of our strength, and the
   very instant that our usefulness has come to an end, we are
   slaughtered with hideous cruelty.

   No animal is free. The life of an animal is misery and
   slavery: that is the plain truth.

   But is this simply part of the order of nature? Is it because
   this land of ours is so poor that it cannot afford a decent

life to those who dwell upon it? No, comrades, a thousand times no!

Why then do we continue in this miserable condition? Because nearly the whole of the produce of our labour is stolen from us by human beings. There, comrades, is the answer to all our problems. It is summed up in a single word – Man. Man is the only real enemy we have. Remove Man from the scene, and the root cause of hunger and overwork is abolished forever.

Man is the only creature that consumes without producing. He does not give milk. He does not lay eggs, he is too weak to pull the plough, he cannot run fast enough to catch rabbits. Yet he is the lord of all the animals. He sets them to work, he gives back to them the bare minimum that will prevent them from starving and the rest he keeps for himself.

Is it not crystal clear then, comrades, that all the evils of this life of ours spring from the tyranny of human beings? Only get rid of Man and the produce of labour would be our own. Almost overnight we could become rich and free. What then must we do? Why, work night and day, body and soul, for the overthrow of the human race. That is my message to you comrades. Revolution!

I do not know when the Revolution will come, it might be in a week or in a hundred years, but I know that sooner or later justice will be done. Fix your eyes on that, comrades, throughout the short remainder of your lives. And above all, pass on this message of mine to those who come after you, so that future generations shall carry on the struggle until it is victorious.

And remember, comrades, your resolution must never falter. No argument must lead you astray. Never listen when they tell you that Man and the animals have a common interest, that the prosperity of the one is the prosperity of the other. It is all lies. Man serves the interests of no creature except himself. And among us animals let there be perfect unity, perfect comradeship in the struggle. All animals are comrades.

I have little more to say. I merely repeat, remember always
your duty of enmity towards Man and all his ways. Whatever goes upon two legs is an enemy. Whatever goes upon
four legs or has wings is a friend. And remember also that in
fighting against Man, we must not come to resemble him.
Even when you have conquered him, do not adopt his vices.
No animal must ever live in a house, or sleep in a bed, or
wear clothes, or drink alcohol, or smoke tobacco, or touch
money, or engage in trade. All the habits of Man are evil. And,
above all, no animal must ever tyrannize over his own kind.
Weak or strong, clever or simple, we are all brothers. No
animal must ever kill any other animal. All animals are equal.

And now, comrades, I will tell you about my dream last
night. I cannot describe that dream to you. It was a dream
of the earth as it will be when Man has vanished. But it
reminded me of something that I had long forgotten. Many
years ago my mother used to sing an old song of which she
knew only the tune and the first three words. I had known
that tune in my infancy, but it had long since passed out of
my mind. Last night, however, it came back to me in my
dream – and what is more, the words of the song also came
back – words, I am certain, which were sung by animals of
long ago and have been lost to memory for generations.
I will sing you that song now, comrades, and when I have
taught you the tune you can sing it better for yourselves.
It is called 'Beasts of England'.

Beasts of England, beasts of Ireland,
Beasts of every land and clime,
Hearken to my joyful tidings
Of the golden future time.

Soon or late the day is coming,
Tyrant Man shall be o'erthrown,
And the fruitful fields of England
Shall be trod by beasts alone.

Bright will shine the fields of England,
Purer shall its waters be,
Sweeter yet shall blow its breezes
On the day that sets us free.

For that day we all must labour,
Though we die before it break;
Cows and horses, geese and turkeys,
All must toil for freedom's sake.

Beasts of England, beasts of Ireland,
Beasts of every land and clime,
Hearken well and spread my tidings
Of the golden future time.

The ANIMALS *learn the song.*

The sound of JONES*'s gun interrupts the singing.*

STORYTELLER. Three nights later old Major died peacefully in his sleep.

During the next three months there was much secret activity. The work of teaching and organising everybody was done by the pigs, who were the cleverest of the animals. The three most important pigs were Snowball, Napoleon and Squealer who began to develop a system of thought based on what old Major had said. They called it Animalism. And then there was Moses, the tame raven, who was Mr Jones's special pet.

MOSES. Yeah, hallelujah, gather round brothers and sisters. We're all gonna live on Sugarcandy Mountain. Up there friends, up there, just on the other side of the dark clouds, there lies Sugarcandy Mountain, that happy country where we poor animals shall rest forever from our labours. After we die, I say after we die, we gonna live in that land, where it's Sunday seven days a week, clover is in season all the year round and lump sugar and linseed cake grow on the hedges.

STORYTELLER. And of late Mr Jones had taken to drinking more than was good for him, so that he sat all day in his chair in the kitchen reading the newspapers and neglecting the animals.

The Revolution takes place. MR JONES *is expelled from Manor Farm.*

SQUEALER. Silence for Comrade Napoleon!

NAPOLEON. Comrades. Comrades. Jones has gone. The Revolution marks our first step on the road to freedom. The farm, our farm, hitherto known as Manor Farm is now to be called Animal Farm!

SQUEALER. Silence for Comrade Snowball!

SNOWBALL. Comrades, during the past three months we have taught ourselves to read and write, and have succeeded in reducing the principles of Animalism to Seven Commandments which from now on will form the law by which we all shall live.

The Seven Commandments are as follows:

The Commandments are revealed at the back.

SNOWBALL *reads out the Commandments and the* ANIMALS *recite them.*

1. Whatever goes upon two legs is an enemy.
2. Whatever goes upon four legs, or has wings, is a friend.
3. No animal shall wear clothes.
4. No animal shall sleep in a bed.
5. No animal shall drink alcohol.
6. No animal shall kill any other animal.
7. All animals are equal.

SNOWBALL. Now, comrades, to the hayfield. Let us make it a point of honour to get in the harvest more quickly than Jones and his men could do.

A bucket of milk arrives.

MOLLIE. What is going to happen to all that milk? Jones used to mix some of it in our food.

NAPOLEON. Never mind the milk, comrades. That will be attended to. The harvest is more important. Comrade Boxer will lead the way. I shall follow in a few minutes. Forward comrades!

STORYTELLER. So the animals trooped down to the hayfield to begin the harvest. And when Mollie came back in the evening:

MOLLIE. Where's the milk gone?

STORYTELLER. Mollie – the white mare who drew Mr Jones's trap.

MOLLIE. Will there still be sugar now that the Revolution has happened?

SNOWBALL. No, we have no means of making sugar on this farm. Besides, you do not need sugar, you will have all the oats and hay you want.

MOLLIE. And shall I still be allowed to wear ribbons?

SNOWBALL. Comrade, those ribbons that you are devoted to are the badge of slavery. Can you not understand that liberty is worth more than ribbons?

MOLLIE. But can't I keep this pretty blue ribbon I found in the farmhouse?

SNOWBALL. Ribbons should be considered as clothes which are the mark of a human being.

BOXER *flings his hat away.*

STORYTELLER. Boxer the carthorse – his personal motto:

BOXER. I *will* work harder!

MOLLIE. And what happened to the milk? And what's going to happen to the apples from the orchard that you have said are for your use only?

NAPOLEON. Squealer!

SQUEALER. Comrades, you do not imagine, I hope, that we pigs are doing this in a spirit of selfishness and privilege? Many of us actually dislike milk and apples, I dislike them myself. Our sole object in taking these things is to preserve our health. Milk and apples, this has been proved by science comrades, contain substances absolutely necessary to the well-being of a pig. We pigs are brain-workers. The whole management and organisation of this farm depends on us. Day and night we are watching over your welfare. It is for your sake that we drink the milk and eat the apples.

Do you know what would happen if we pigs failed in our duty? Jones would come back! Surely, comrades – surely there is no one among you who would want Jones to come back?

BOXER. What happened at the meeting?

MOLLIE. Why weren't you there?

BOXER. I was working hard at getting the harvest in. I forgot about the meeting and I didn't realise you had all gone.

MOLLIE. Well, that's a pity. You'll just have to try and be on time in future.

CLOVER. Mollie . . .

STORYTELLER. Clover the mare – Boxer's workmate.

BOXER. So, tell me what happened. Did Comrade Napoleon speak?

MOLLIE. No, Squealer did.

BOXER. And what did he say? Oh, please, you must tell me.

CLOVER. Mollie asked about the milk and the apples, which the pigs are keeping for themselves.

MOLLIE. And the lumps of sugar from the farmhouse.

CLOVER. And Squealer said the pigs need those things to help them run the farm better.

BOXER. Is that true?

MOLLIE. No, of course it isn't. It's absolute rubbish.

BOXER. No, really, is that what Squealer said?

CLOVER. Yes, if they don't have the milk and apples they won't be able to think properly, and then Jones might come back.

MOLLIE. He always gives me sugar.

BOXER. Oh, we don't want that.

MOLLIE. And he let me wear pretty ribbons.

CLOVER. No. So we all agreed that it was best if all the milk and apples were saved for the pigs.

MOLLIE. One blue, one red, one green . . .

BOXER. And do you think that's right Clover?

CLOVER. Well, everyone agreed so it must be.

BOXER. Was Comrade Napoleon there?

CLOVER. Yes.

BOXER. And did he agree?

CLOVER. Yes, he asked Squealer to speak in the first place.

BOXER. Oh, well, if Comrade Napoleon says it then it must be right.

MOLLIE. Honestly Boxer, you are stupid, why do you have to agree with everything he says?

BOXER. Well, he's the cleverest animal on the farm, isn't he? So he must . . .

MOLLIE. Who says so? Benjamin's clever, Moses was clever, and so was Mrs Jones, she used to let me have ribbons all the time.

CLOVER. Oh, Mollie, stop going on about your ribbons. You looked silly in them anyway.

MOLLIE. I did not. I'm not silly. At least I'm better at reading and writing than you are Boxer, and you Clover.

CLOVER. Boxer works harder than any of us. He doesn't have much time to learn to read and write.

MOLLIE. How much of your A.B.C. can you say, Boxer? I bet you can't get as far as I can. I can get up to M which starts my name.

BOXER. I can say a bit

MOLLIE. Go on then, let's hear it.

BOXER. A.B.C.

MOLLIE. There you are see . . .

CLOVER. Give him a chance, let him have a think.

BOXER. A.B.C . . .

MOLLIE. A.B.C.D.E.F.G . . .

CLOVER. Mollie, Mollie!

SNOWBALL. Comrades, since some of you have had difficulty in learning to read and write, we have decided to reduce the Commandments of Animalism to a single easily remembered maxim – FOUR LEGS GOOD, TWO LEGS BAD

The ANIMALS *recite the maxim.*

Can the sheep remember it?

The SHEEP *recite the maxim.*

STORYTELLER. Early in October news arrived that Jones and all his men were coming up the track that led to the farm.

Snowball . . .

SNOWBALL. Who had studied an old book of Julius Caesar's campaigns.

STORYTELLER. Gave his orders quickly.

The Battle of the Cowshed takes place.

SNOWBALL. Comrades, the enemy has been repelled, we have won a great victory! But let us not forget, comrades, on this joyful occasion that all animals must be ready to die for Animal Farm if need be.

NAPOLEON. It has been decided comrades to create a military decoration – 'Animal Hero, First Class'– which we confer on Snowball and Boxer, for their valiant efforts in the Battle of the Cowshed.

CLOVER. Mollie, I have something very serious to say to you. This morning I saw you looking over the hedge at the end of the long meadow. There was a man standing on the other side of the hedge and I was a long way away, but I am almost certain I saw this – he was talking to you and you were allowing him to stroke your nose. What does that mean Mollie?

MOLLIE. He didn't, I wasn't, it isn't true!

CLOVER. Mollie, look me in the face, do you give me your word of honour that the man was not stroking your nose.

MOLLIE. It isn't true!

STORYTELLER. Three days later Mollie disappeared. Nothing was heard of her until one day a pigeon reported . . .

PIGEON. I saw her, between the shafts of a smart trap painted red and black outside a pub. A fat red-faced man was stroking her nose and feeding her with sugar, and she wore a scarlet ribbon round her forelock. She looked as if she was enjoying herself.

STORYTELLER. None of the animals ever mentioned Mollie again.

NAPOLEON. That's all very well, Comrade Snowball, but I still maintain sowing a bigger acreage of oats will serve us better through the winter and that the soil on the hillside is more suitable for root vegetables.

STORYTELLER. Another meeting, another argument between Napoleon and Snowball.

SNOWBALL. But Comrade Napoleon you still haven't heard the most important part of my plan yet.

NAPOLEON. Oh yes, what's that?

SNOWBALL. The building of a windmill . . .

NAPOLEON. A what?

SNOWBALL. A machine operated by the wind to generate electricity and make life easier for all of us. The small hill in the long pasture is the highest point on the farm, right? After surveying the ground I have decided that it's the best place to build a windmill, which could be made to operate a dynamo and supply the farm with electrical power. This could be used to light our stalls and keep them warm in winter. It could also run a circular saw, a chaff cutter, a mangel-slicer and an electrical milking machine. This farm is old-fashioned, we have only primitive machinery. The power of a windmill would make our work so much easier, and leave us free to pursue more noble tasks.

NAPOLEON. Well, comrades, how do we feel about Snowball's plan?

SNOWBALL. I'm not saying it will be easy – we shall have to quarry stone and build walls, make the sails and find dynamos and cables. But I calculate that the whole thing could be finished in a year, and after that so much labour will be saved that we will only need to work three days a week. Think of that, comrades.

NAPOLEON. And I say that the year would be better spent increasing food production. That is our greatest need at the moment. If we waste time building a windmill, we will all starve to death.

CLOVER. Vote for Snowball and the three-day week!

SQUEALER. Vote for Napoleon and the full manger!

An argument ensues.

NAPOLEON. Comrades, comrades – let us not argue. Let us vote on the matter, and abide by the decision of the majority. Now, I think that this windmill idea is a piece of nonsense, and I advise you all to vote against it.

SNOWBALL. Let us rid ourselves of the chains of sordid labour. Electricity can do that for us. Just picture our lives when the wonders of science have freed us from our daily toil. The windmill will operate threshing machines, ploughs, harrows, rollers, reapers and binders, besides supplying every stall with light, hot and cold water and a heater. Let us move forward, comrades, to an age of true freedom. Let us forge the future of Animal Farm in the white heat of technology!

At a sign from NAPOLEON, the DOGS expel SNOWBALL from the farm.

NAPOLEON. From now on, comrades, the weekly meetings
will come to an end. They are unnecessary and a waste of
time. In future, all questions relating to the working of the
farm will be settled by a special committee of pigs presided
over by myself. The meetings will be held in private, and
you will assemble once a week to be given your orders, but
there will be no more debates. Minimus, you young porker,
come with me.

SQUEALER. Comrades, I trust that every animal here
appreciates the sacrifice that Comrade Napoleon has made
in taking this extra labour upon himself. Do not imagine,
comrades, that leadership is a pleasure – on the contrary,
it is a deep and heavy responsibility. No one believes more
firmly than Comrade Napoleon that all animals are equal.
He would be only too happy to let you make your decisions
for yourselves. But sometimes you might make the wrong
decision, comrades, and then where should we be?

Suppose you had decided to follow Snowball with his
moonshine of windmills – Snowball, who, as we now know,
was no better than a criminal.

BOXER. He fought bravely at the Battle of the Cowshed.

SQUEALER. Bravery is not enough. Loyalty and obedience
are more important. And as to the Battle of the Cowshed,
I believe the time will come when we shall find that
Snowball's part in it was much exaggerated. Discipline,
comrades, iron discipline! That is the watchword for today.
One false step and our enemies would be upon us. Surely,
comrades, you do not want Jones back? Very well then, let
Comrade Napoleon's dedication be a shining example to us
all. Was it not he, after all, who said: 'All the habits of Man
are evil, and above all, no animal must ever tyrannize over
his own kind'?

BOXER. If the holding of meetings means that Jones will
come back, then there must be no more meetings. Comrade
Napoleon says it, so it must be right.

SQUEALER. Oh, he does, comrades, he does. And one other
thing, comrades, Napoleon has decided to go ahead with the

plans to build the windmill. Now this will need a very special effort from all of you, as we will have to carry on running the farm while the windmill is being constructed. It might even be necessary to reduce your rations. I can understand your surprise, comrades, but you see Napoleon has never really been opposed to the building of a windmill. In fact, the idea was his own creation in the first place, and Snowball stole it only to make himself look clever in your eyes.

CLOVER. Why then did Napoleon speak so strongly against it at the meeting?

SQUEALER. Ah, that was Comrade Napoleon's cunning. He appeared to oppose the windmill, only to get rid of Snowball, who was a dangerous character and a bad influence. Now that Snowball is out of the way, we can get on with the job. That, comrades, is what is known as tactics. Tactics, comrades, tactics.

BOXER. Napoleon is always right.

The building of the windmill begins.

NAPOLEON. All animals will work a sixty hour week, and in future there will be work on Sunday afternoon as well. This work will be strictly voluntary, of course, but any animal not reporting for work will have his rations cut by half.

In addition, comrades, Animal Farm will begin to engage in trade with the neighbouring farm, not, of course, for any commercial purpose, but simply to obtain essential materials such as paraffin oil, nails, string and iron for the horses' shoes. Therefore, I am making arrangements to sell a stack of hay, part of the current year's wheat crop, and, if necessary, a percentage of the egg yield to a neighbouring farm. You should welcome this contribution towards the building of the windmill. And have no fear, there will be no need for any of you to come into contact with human beings which would be most undesirable. I shall take that burden upon myself, and make all the arrangements.

BENJAMIN. 'Ere . . .

STORYTELLER. Benjamin, the donkey –

BENJAMIN. 'Ere, didn't we pass a resolution sometime back about not having nothing to do with human beings and not engaging in trade?

BOXER. I can't remember that.

BENJAMIN. And about money, we're not supposed to handle money.

BOXER. I don't know about that Benjamin, stop being so miserable. Aren't you happier now that Mr Jones has gone?

BENJAMIN. I don't see anything to laugh at. Donkeys live a long time. None of you has ever seen a dead donkey. God gave me a tail to keep the flies off, but I'd sooner have no tail and no flies . . .

CLOVER. I think Benjamin may be right. I seem to remember when old Major first spoke to us on that historic night he mentioned something about money.

BOXER. Look Clover, I don't remember anything about that. I've told you before, don't listen to Benjamin. He's a nice enough fellow and he does his work alright, but he's always grumbling and going around the place looking gloomy.

CLOVER. Yes I know, but he's often right about things. He's older than the rest of us, he can remember everything, and he can read much better than you or I can.

BOXER. What's that got to do with it?

CLOVER. Well, nothing really.

BOXER. I work as hard as I possibly can. I get up an hour earlier in the morning, and often work in the evening. We've got to get the windmill finished. I haven't got time to look at books, and learn to read and write. It's what you're best at that counts.

CLOVER. Yes, of course, Boxer, nobody works harder than you, and we all respect you for it. I didn't mean to upset you. I believe in the Revolution, and the work that Napoleon is doing as much as you do. It's just that sometimes things don't seem to happen the way that Major said they would.

BOXER. We mustn't think too hard about it Clover. We must trust Napoleon, he knows best.

CLOVER. I'm sure you're right.

SQUEALER. Penny for them, Comrade Boxer?

BOXER. Clover and I were just discussing Comrade Napoleon's speech on trade.

SQUEALER. And what conclusions did you come to?

BOXER. Oh, that he's right of course. It's just that old Benjamin, you know how he is, seemed to think we'd passed some resolution about not talking to humans or trading with them. And Clover . . .

SQUEALER. Yes . . .

CLOVER. I thought he might be right.

SQUEALER. Are you certain that this is not something you have dreamed, comrades? You only imagine that we passed these resolutions because of the lies spread about by that traitor Snowball. Have you any record of them? Are they written down anywhere? No, of course they aren't, so let us all carry on with our work, and leave Comrade Napoleon to worry about these other things.

BOXER. There you are you see. Comrade Napoleon is always right. If he thinks it's best that we should sell things, then that is what we should do.

CLOVER. Yes, I know, but I'm sure it's not a good idea to have anything to do with human beings. Major did warn us about that, and what he said then should guide us in what we do now.

BOXER. He isn't here anymore. If he was, he'd agree with Napoleon.

CLOVER. That's something we'll never know.

BOXER. No, of course not.

CLOVER. But Benjamin does have a good memory.

BOXER. Oh, don't start on about him again. 'Have you ever seen a dead donkey,' indeed. 'I'd sooner have no tail and no flies.' All the time. I don't know what he's going on about. If you ask me, all that thinking has made him a bit soft in the head.

CLOVER. But I'm not asking you, I'm just saying I think he may be right.

BOXER. Maybe, might, I'm not sure – you're as bad as he is, talking in riddles. Come on, back to work, that'll solve everything.

CLOVER. Oh Boxer!

BENJAMIN. I've seen them!

CLOVER. What?

BENJAMIN. I said I've seen them.

BOXER. Who?

BENJAMIN. Napoleon, Squealer and all the other pigs. They've moved into the farmhouse. They're living there.

BOXER. I don't believe you.

BENJAMIN. But it's true I tell you. I looked through the kitchen window, and there was Squealer sitting in a chair with his legs up on the table, reading a newspaper.

BOXER. I simply don't believe you.

BENJAMIN. I saw it. And all the other pigs were sitting around the table, munching apples and drinking milk.

CLOVER. Are you sure?

BENJAMIN. Of course I'm sure. I know what I've seen.

CLOVER. Well, I think that's going a bit too far, don't you Boxer?

BOXER. Well, maybe they need to be in the farmhouse, so that . . .

BENJAMIN. But that's not all, one of the pigeons flew past the upstairs windows of the farmhouse yesterday, and you'll never guess what she saw – Go on, tell them what you saw . . .

PIGEON. Well, in the big room where Mr and Mrs Jones used to sleep in the big bed – Napoleon was stretched out on the bed fast asleep and snoring very loudly.

BENJAMIN. There, you see.

BOXER. How could you see all this if you flew past the window?

PIGEON. I didn't only fly past, comrade, I perched on the windowsill and had a good look.

CLOVER. And saw Napoleon asleep in the bed and heard him snoring?

PIGEON. Yes, comrade, the window was open.

CLOVER. When was this?

PIGEON. About two hours ago, comrade.

BOXER. Napoleon needs to rest. He works very hard for all of us. He'd probably been working late last night and got tired.

BENJAMIN. But he was sleeping in a bed.

BOXER. Well, so what?

BENJAMIN. The Fourth Commandment!

SQUEALER *'adjusts' the Fourth Commandment.*

BOXER. What?

CLOVER. Yes, of course, Boxer, Benjamin's right. The Fourth Commandment says, 'No animal shall sleep in a bed.' So, if Comrade Napoleon's sleeping in one, it's only right that we should tell the others.

BOXER. Oh, I don't know about that.

BENJAMIN. Stop being so stubborn Boxer.

BOXER. Well, you leave me out of it, I don't want to cause any trouble. I just want to get on with my work. You talk to them Clover, if you like. Nobody ever listens to me. You bring it up at the next meeting.

CLOVER. I'm not very good at talking in front of all the others. Benjamin, it would be best if you did it.

BENJAMIN. No, they'll listen to you. If you start it off, I'll support you.

BOXER. You be careful Clover, don't get mixed up in something which is going to upset things . . .

CLOVER. Benjamin read the Fourth Commandment.

BENJAMIN. It says – 'No animal shall sleep in a bed . . . with sheets.'

SQUEALER. So, comrades, you have heard that we pigs are now sleeping in the beds of the farmhouse? And why not? You did not suppose, surely, that there was ever a ruling against beds. A bed merely means a place to sleep in. A pile of straw in a stall is a bed, properly regarded. The rule was against sheets which are a human invention. We have removed the sheets from the farmhouse beds, and sleep between blankets. And very comfortable they are too! But not more comfortable than we need, I can tell you, comrades, with all the brainwork we have to do nowadays. You would not have us too tired to carry out our duties. Surely none of you wishes to see Jones back? Well?

CLOVER, BENJAMIN *and* BOXER. No, comrade.

SQUEALER. Very well then. Because he will come back, I assure you, if we are not left to get on with our work in peace and quiet. Oh, one other thing, from now on we'll be getting up one hour later in the mornings than the rest of you, OK?

BOXER. There you see, I told you not to meddle.

STORYTELLER. November came with strong winds and torrential rains. Finally there came a night when the gale was so violent that the main buildings rocked on their foundations and several tiles were blown off the roof of the barn. In the morning, when the animals woke up, a terrible sight met their eyes.

The ANIMALS *gather at the ruined windmill.*

SQUEALER. Comrades, do you know who is responsible for this? Do you know the enemy who has come in the night and overthrown our windmill? Snowball. Snowball has done this thing, to set back our plans and avenge himself for his ignominious expulsion. This traitor has crept here under cover of night and destroyed our work of nearly a year. Comrades, here and now I pronounce the death sentence upon Snowball. 'Animal Hero, Second Class' to any animal who brings him to justice.

NAPOLEON. No more delays, comrades, there is work to be done. This very morning we begin re-building the windmill and we will build all through the winter, rain or shine. We will teach this miserable traitor that he cannot undo our work so easily. Remember, comrades, there must be no alteration in our plans; they shall be carried out to the day. Forward, comrades – Long live the windmill. Long live Animal Farm!

ANIMAL 1. He visits the farm at night. I've seen him.

ANIMAL 2. Who?

ANIMAL 3. Snowball, of course. He must have stolen all that corn which went missing two days ago.

ANIMAL 1. Yes, and broken all those eggs, which were ready for market.

ANIMAL 3. He's taken the key to the store-shed and thrown it down the well.

ANIMAL 1. He's stolen the apples from the orchard.

ANIMAL 2. Broken windows.

ANIMAL 3. Destroyed fences.

ANIMAL 1. Poisoned the milk.

ANIMAL 2. Blocked the drains.

ANIMAL 3. Uprooted the crops.

ANIMAL 1. Throttled the chickens.

SQUEALER. And generally proved himself to be the swine that he always was. Comrades! A most terrible thing has been discovered. Snowball was in league with Jones from the very start. He was Jones's secret agent all the time. It has all been proved by documents which he left behind him and which we have only just discovered. To my mind this explains a great deal, comrades. Did we not see for ourselves how he attempted, fortunately without success, to get us defeated and destroyed at the Battle of the Cowshed?

BOXER. I do not believe that. Snowball fought bravely at the Battle of the Cowshed – I saw him myself. Did we not give him 'Animal Hero, First Class' immediately afterwards?

SQUEALER. That was our mistake, comrade, for we now know, it is all written down in the secret documents that we have found, that in reality he was trying to lure us to our doom.

BOXER. But he was wounded. We all saw him running with blood.

SQUEALER. That was all part of the arrangement. I could show you this in his own writing if you were able to read it, but you can't, so I won't. He would have succeeded if it had not been for our heroic Leader, Comrade Napoleon. Do you not remember how, just at the moment when Jones and his men had got inside the yard, Snowball suddenly turned and fled and many animals followed him? And do you remember too, that it was just at that moment when panic was spreading and all seemed lost, that Comrade Napoleon sprang forward with a cry of 'Death to Humanity', and sank his teeth in Jones's leg – surely you remember that, comrades?

BOXER. I do not believe that Snowball was a traitor at the beginning. What he has done since is different. But I believe that at the Battle of the Cowshed, he was a good comrade.

SQUEALER. Our Leader, Comrade Napoleon, has stated categorically – categorically, comrade – that Snowball was Jones's agent from the very beginning – yes, and from long before the Revolution was ever thought of.

BOXER. Ah, that is different. If Comrade Napoleon says it, it
must be right.

SQUEALER. That is the true spirit, comrade. I warn every
animal on the farm to keep their eyes very wide open, for
we have reason to think that some of Snowball's agents are
lurking among us at the moment.

NAPOLEON. And we shall seek out those traitors in our
midst, comrades. They will confess their crimes and be
punished accordingly. Have you anything to confess?

FOUR PIGS. We have secretly been in touch with Snowball
ever since his expulsion. We collaborated with him to
destroy the windmill, and were planning to help him hand
over Animal Farm to a neighbouring farm.

NAPOLEON. And . . .

FOUR PIGS. Snowball admitted to us that he had been Jones's
secret agent for four years.

The FOUR PIGS *are executed.*

NAPOLEON. Does any other animal have anything to
confess?

THREE GEESE. Snowball persuaded us to steal corn and hand
it over to him.

Execution.

TWO SHEEP. Snowball visited us at night and encouraged us
to poison the drinking water.

Execution.

ONE HEN. Snowball appeared to me in a dream and incited
me to disobey your orders.

Execution.

CLOVER *begins to sing 'Beasts of England'.*

SQUEALER *'adjusts' the Sixth Commandment.*

BOXER. I do not understand it. I would not have believed that
such things could happen on our farm. It must be due to

some fault in ourselves. The solution, as I see it, is to work harder.

SQUEALER. By a special decree of Comrade Napoleon, 'Beasts of England' has been abolished. It is now forbidden to sing it.

CLOVER. Why?

SQUEALER. It is no longer needed, comrade. 'Beasts of England' was the song of the Revolution. But the Revolution is now completed. The execution of the traitors was the final act. The enemy both external and internal has been defeated. In 'Beasts of England' we expressed our longing for a better society in days to come. But that society has now been established. Clearly this song has no longer any purpose. In its place, Minimus the poet has composed a new song which begins:

MINIMUS.
Animal Farm, Animal Farm,
Never through me shalt thou
Come to harm!

BENJAMIN. Well, I don't think much of that, the tune's not the same somehow.

CLOVER. The Sixth Commandment. 'No animal shall kill any other animal.' Benjamin read me the Sixth Commandment.

BENJAMIN. No!

CLOVER. Oh, please, it's important.

BENJAMIN. No, I read you the fourth one last time and that didn't help.

CLOVER. But I'm sure I'm right this time. I can remember seeing Snowball write it up there.

BENJAMIN. Who?

CLOVER. Snowball, oh you remember. It comes after 'No animal shall drink alcohol'. I've said them to myself often enough. Oh, please read it for me. After what happened I'm very confused now. Comrade Napoleon is always right of course, but I thought we were working together and . . .

BENJAMIN. 'No animal shall kill any other animal . . . without cause.'

CLOVER. Oh.

The building of the windmill continues as MINIMUS *recites his poem.*

MINIMUS
Friend of the fatherless!
Fountain of happiness!
Lord of the swill-bucket! Oh, how my soul is on
Fire when I gaze at thy
Calm and commanding eye,
Like the sun in the sky,
Comrade Napoleon!

Thou art the giver of
All that thy creatures love,
Full belly twice a day, clean straw to roll upon;
Every beast great or small
Sleeps at peace in his stall,
Thou watchest over all,
Comrade Napoleon!

Had I a sucking-pig,
Ere he had grown as big
Even as a pint bottle or a rolling-pin,
He should have learned to be
Faithful and true to thee,
Yes, his first squeak should be
'Comrade Napoleon!'

BOXER. Please inform our Leader, Comrade Napoleon, that the windmill is now completed.

NAPOLEON. It is fitting, comrades, that on this historic day we should proclaim that Animal Farm is now a Republic.

SQUEALER. And announce that our Leader, Comrade Napoleon, has been unanimously elected as its first President.

A new decoration, The Order of the Green Banner, has been created to mark the occasion and President Napoleon is its first recipient.

A 'Spontaneous Demonstration' takes place.

NAPOLEON. We have won a great victory, comrades, and are now truly our own masters. The building of the windmill, which will be marked by an anniversary each year, serves to remind us that through our own efforts we can control our destiny. But this wonderful effort should not give rise to complacency. The struggle must go on, we must work even harder. The windmill will not be used to generate electricity, but to grind corn, which should yield a handsome profit. We shall build another windmill, comrades, and when that one is finished, we shall install the dynamos. But the changes which the traitor Snowball – who as we all know was Jones's agent before the Revolution, and fought on Jones's side at the Battle of the Cowshed – the changes which he talked about, namely electric light and heat, will not take place, because they are contrary to the spirit of Animalism. The truest happiness lies in working hard and living frugally. Each animal will receive a special gift of a slice of apple in recognition of his efforts. Forward, comrades, forward in the name of the Revolution. LONG LIVE ANIMAL FARM!

STORYTELLER. And then, out of the blue, Moses returned.

MOSES. Yeah, comrades, in my absence I have been away, and where have I been, comrades? Where have I been? Well, I'll tell you where I've been – I have been to Sugarcandy Mountain and I have seen the glory of that lovely land. I have been high above the clouds and seen the beauty of that place where we all one day shall rest our weary limbs in everlasting peace.

CLOVER. Tell us about it Moses, tell us about it.

BENJAMIN. Don't listen to our flighty friend. It's just a load of bull. There is no such place, when you're dead, you're dead.

CLOVER. But our lives here are hard and we are hungry most of the time. We sleep, we work, we sleep, we work. There's no end to it.

MOSES. You are right to chastise the hoofer. As I was saying, comrades, Sugarcandy Mountain is more beautiful than we can ever imagine. For I have seen the everlasting fields of clover, where the sun shines on and on, and no cloud dares show its face. I have seen the linseed cake growing on the hedges and I'm telling you I have seen the lumps of sugar hanging in bunches from the trees. And we're all gonna go there, comrades, we're gonna be there together. We're gonna live on Sugarcandy Mountain. Put your hands together comrades, sing your hearts out, let's hear it for Sugarcandy Mountain.

The ANIMALS *sing and sway.*

The singing is interrupted by the sound of drunken revelry from the farmhouse. NAPOLEON *and* SQUEALER *enter and hastily exit in an alcoholic stupor.* SQUEALER *re-enters to 'adjust' the Fifth Commandment.*

MOSES. Come on, comrades, sing your hearts out – We're gonna live on Sugarcandy Mountain.

CLOVER. What's the matter Benjamin?

BENJAMIN (*reading the Commandment*). 'No animal shall drink alcohol . . . to excess.'

The singing goes quiet.

SQUEALER. For the time being, comrades, it has been found necessary to make readjustments of rations. From tomorrow all animals other than pigs will receive two pounds less corn a day and no carrots on Sundays. This is being done in an effort to rationalise present food supplies. Remember, comrades, that a too-rigid equality in rations would be contrary to the principles of Animalism. And let us remind ourselves that in comparison with times before the Revolution, we have made enormous improvements. Working hours have been reduced by 30%, our drinking water is of better quality, 45% more young ones survive infancy, the average life of an animal is longer by 25%, animal literacy is up 630%, incidents of foot and mouth disease, foulpest and mange reduced by 85%, and glanders almost completely eradicated, production of milk is up 35.5%, of eggs 43.25%, and of wool 53.85%.

BOXER *collapses.*

SQUEALER *observes and hurriedly exits.*

CLOVER. Boxer, what is it?

BOXER *breathes heavily.*

SQUEALER *returns.*

SQUEALER. Comrade Boxer, I can't tell you how distressed I am to see you like this. I have already informed Comrade Napoleon of your condition and he has instructed me to communicate to you his deepest personal sympathy, and his best wishes for a speedy recovery. You have always been one of the most loyal workers on the farm, and even at this moment, Comrade Napoleon is making arrangements to send you to be treated at a hospital nearby. The vet there can treat you far better than we can.

CLOVER. In a hospital? But no animal has ever left the farm before.

BENJAMIN. Except Snowball.

CLOVER. We'll look after him.

SQUEALER. Nonsense, comrades, nonsense! I can understand your concern, but the plain truth is that we do not have the facilities here to provide Boxer with the treatment he must have if he is to make a complete recovery. The van will be arriving shortly to take him away.

CLOVER. If Boxer rests for a couple of days, I know he'll be strong again.

SQUEALER. There is no argument! Our Leader, Comrade Napoleon, has said quite definitely that Boxer is to go to hospital for the good of his health.

BOXER. Oh well, if Comrade Napoleon says it, it must be right.

CLOVER *and* BENJAMIN *help* BOXER *to his feet.*

Thanks, comrades. Don't worry about me. I'm glad I was able to see the windmill finished at any rate. To tell you the truth, I'm looking forward to retiring. I'd only a month to go anyway. I'll have time to study a bit, learn the rest of the alphabet. You're getting on a bit too, Benjamin, maybe they'll let you retire too and keep me company. You get an apple on Sundays, just like the pigs.

BOXER *says goodbye to* CLOVER *and* BENJAMIN.

The van arrives.

BENJAMIN. Fools, fools, do you not see what is written on the side of the van – 'Alfred Simmonds, Horse Slaughterer'. They are sending Boxer away to be killed.

CLOVER. Boxer! Boxer! Get out, get out quickly, they are taking you to your death!

BOXER *is taken away.*

STORYTELLER. Boxer was never seen again, and three days later . . .

SQUEALER. Comrades, in spite of receiving every attention a horse could have, Boxer has died in the hospital. I was there during his last hours, and I can honestly say it was one of the most affecting sights I have ever seen. At the end, almost too weak to speak, he whispered in my ear that his sole sorrow was to have passed on when there was still so much work to be done. 'Forward comrades,' he whispered, 'forward in the name of the Revolution. Long live Comrade Napoleon. Napoleon is always right.' Those were his last words.

NAPOLEON. Ideas which every animal would do well to adopt as his own, comrades. Let the spirit of Boxer be a shining example to us all in the difficult times that lie ahead. He was a true son of the Revolution, and it is all the more shameful therefore that his passing should have been marked by the spreading of rumours that he was being taken away to the slaughterhouse.

Some of you read 'Horse Slaughterer' on the side of the van and jumped to the conclusion that Boxer was being taken away to be killed. It is almost unbelievable that any animal could be so stupid. Surely you know me better than that. The explanation is really very simple. The van previously belonged to the slaughterer, who sold it to the vet. Comrade Boxer died receiving the best care and attention that money could provide. I personally gave the order that no expense was to be spared. Unfortunately it has not been possible to bring back our lamented comrade's remains for internment on the farm, but I have ordered a large wreath to be made from laurels and sent down to be placed on Boxer's grave. Let us cherish his memory, comrades, in our daily lives, and pledge ourselves to work harder for the prosperity of Animal Farm as a tribute to him.

MOSES. And have no fear, comrades, for I know that even now Comrade Boxer is cropping the grass on Sugarcandy Mountain and resting his weary limbs on those sunlit pastures.

CLOVER. Really, Moses? Is he up there now?

MOSES. Why yes, indeed he is, sister, and we should all rejoice for him, and you all remember now that we're gonna join him there after we die. I say, after we die, we're gonna live on Sugar . . .

NAPOLEON. Squealer!!!

SQUEALER. The latest report on the progress of the farm, comrades, indicates that things are getting better all the time. Annual income has increased by 225% over the last three years, sale of timber has increased money supply to the extent that 15% of our essential materials are now purchased from outside the farm.

This means that the average working day has been reduced by 12% per week over the past six months and leisure time has been increased by 33%. Time spent in educating the young has doubled.

CLOVER. It seems to me that our lives are just the same as they have always been. I try hard to remember what it was like in the days before the Revolution, and then again what it was like after Jones had been expelled. Were things better than they are now? It's so long ago.

YOUNG ANIMAL. What do you mean Revolution? Who was Jones? What does expelled mean? Why are you always wondering if things are better?

CLOVER. You are too young to know. But it's right that you should ask, and I'll tell you what I can remember. The Revolution happened a long, long time ago, and before it happened a man called Jones ruled over us and treated us very badly.

YOUNG ANIMAL. What's a man?

CLOVER. A man is a creature who walks on two legs instead of four. Jones lived in a farmhouse . . .

YOUNG ANIMAL. Where the pigs live now?

CLOVER. Yes, and he fed us and looked after . . .

MOSES. My, my, you tell it to the youngster, Sister Clover, they were fine days to be sure.

SQUEALER. Moses, old chap, do you fancy coming into the farmhouse for a glass of stout? There's something I want to talk to you about.

MOSES. Why, thank you kindly, Comrade Squealer.

CLOVER. And then there came that historic day when Jones was expelled from the farm and we began to rule our own lives.

YOUNG ANIMAL. Was it exciting?

CLOVER. Oh yes, very exciting. I can remember the thrill when we realised we were in charge. When we achieved perfect unity.

YOUNG ANIMAL. And did things get better?

CLOVER. Why yes, of course they did, we were free. We had more . . . we . . .

BENJAMIN. I can remember everything about my life, and I know that things are never much better or much worse. Let's face it, hunger, hardship and disappointment are our lot.

CLOVER. But we mustn't give up hope. It is, after all, an honour and a privilege to be members of Animal Farm, still the only farm in the whole country to be owned and operated by animals. The golden future which old Major promised us and which we used to sing about is still coming. It may not happen in our lifetime, but it will happen. We feed ourselves, we work for ourselves, we serve no man. All animals are equal!

MOSES. Four legs good, two legs better! Four legs good, two legs better! . . .

SQUEALER *and* NAPOLEON *walk on 'two legs'.*

The single Commandment is revealed.

CLOVER. What are you doing?

SQUEALER. We, comrades, work hard all day long writing files, reports, minutes and memoranda.

CLOVER. But then you burn them.

SQUEALER. They are of the highest importance for the welfare of the farm.

CLOVER. But what are they for? I mean what . . . what . . . ?

Benjamin, read the Commandments – are the Seven Commandments the same as they used to be, Benjamin? Oh, please Benjamin, read it for me just once more.

BENJAMIN. 'All animals are equal. But some animals are more equal than others.'

CLOVER. But what does that mean, Benjamin? We're all equal, how can some animals be more equal than others? All that talk, all the facts, all the paper and all the writing make everything so complicated. Too complicated for me to under-stand. I believe in the Revolution and everything that our Leader, Comrade Napoleon, says. Just like Boxer did, and nobody worked harder than him for the cause. I remember in the early days, just after we'd got rid of Jones . . .

She begins to hum 'Beasts of England'.

PILKINGTON. Hello, I said hello, is there anybody there? Dashed odd – could have sworn the invite said seven pm for cocktails. Not a soul to be seen. Just a broken-down old carthorse moaning away. Don't see what these damned pigs have to be so proud of. Hello – name's Pilkington from the farm next door.

NAPOLEON (*off*). Ah, yes old boy. Shan't keep you a moment.

PILKINGTON. Good, thought I might have a look over the old place, whilst I'm waiting.

NAPOLEON (*off*). If you hang on a tick old man, I'll give you a guided tour myself.

PILKINGTON. Ah good, must say it's looking in absolutely splendid nick. I noticed the windmill on the way in. Jolly fine achievement. All those animals working away in the fields, and working jolly hard too. Amazing! Don't pamper them, that's the answer eh? I can see I'll be able to pick up a few tips from this visit.

Yes, well I must say I'm glad we're able to get together like this to talk about mutual problems. It's a source of great satisfaction to me that a long period of mistrust and misunderstanding has now come to an end. There was a time, not that I shared such sentiments, when the respected proprietors of Animal Farm were regarded not exactly with hostility but, shall we say, with a certain measure of misgiving by their neighbours. But now all such doubts have been dispelled. I hope very much that this meeting will mark the start of friendly relations between ourselves.

There is no earthly reason why there should be any clash of interests between pigs and human beings. Your struggles and difficulties are exactly the same as ours. I mean to say, isn't the labour problem the same everywhere? Dare say some of your workers get a bit bolshy at times, eh? Yes, well I know the problem. Just as you have your lower animals to contend with, we have our lower classes, what, ha, ha . . .

The PIGS/MEN *walk on.*

NAPOLEON. Couldn't agree with you more, old boy. It's true we have had our ups and downs in the past, but hopefully all that is now at an end. The rumours that have been spread about us have been truly shocking. For instance, it has been said that we slaughter animals unnecessarily, and want to stir up revolution on other farms. Nothing could be further from the truth! Our sole desire is to live at peace with our neighbours and to carry on trade to our mutual advantage. We own the farm, and to show our good intentions we have decided to abolish the custom of addressing each other as comrade. Can't think how it started in the first place anyway. Our lower animals, as you so rightly put it, Pilkington old chap, work longer hours and receive less food than animals on any other farm. We are justly proud of our achievement. So, gentlemen, I give you a toast.

PILKINGTON. Exactly – to the prosperity of Animal Farm.

NAPOLEON. Wrong old boy, wrong. It is only fitting that the farm should be known henceforth by its correct and original name. So, I give you the toast as before, but in a different form. Lift your glasses, gentlemen, to the prosperity of Manor Farm!

The party swells.

CLOVER *watches in horror.*

The End.